THE U.S. OPEN 2022

Serena Williams Delays Her Retirement with First Round Win

BY

RACHEL JAMES

TABLE OF CONTENTS

BRIEF INTRODUCTION TO THE UNITED STATES OPEN

The US Open, also known as the US Open Tennis Championships, is an international tennis tournament held on hard courts. It is the year's fourth Grand Slam tournament, taking place over two weeks in late August and early September. The Australian Open, French Open, and Wimbledon are the other three Grand Slam tournaments.

Since 1978, all US Open matches have been played on the acrylic hard courts of the US Tennis

Association (USTA) National Tennis Center in Queens, New York, which was renamed in 2006 as the USTA Billie Jean King National Tennis Center. Serena Williams has made the most singles finals appearances in tournament history. Serena Williams has reached the final ten times and won six titles since 1999. Serena Williams and Chris Evert are the two players who have won the most singles titles, with six each.

CHAPTER ONE

<u>Serena Williams Biography</u>

Serena Williams (born September 26, 1981, in Saginaw, Michigan, USA) is an American tennis player who, with her powerful style of play, revolutionized women's tennis and has been awarded Grand Slam singles titles more than any other person in the open era. Williams was raised in Compton, California. Her family consisted of her parents, a nurse named Orcaene Price, and a security guard named Richard Williams, as well as her older sister, Venus Williams. Price had three daughters from a previous marriage as well.

While both Serena and Venus Williams' parents encouraged them to play tennis, it was Richard Williams who primarily taught them the game, taking the two girls to public courts in the area. He was known as a strict coach, and the sisters practiced for long hours. In order for Serena and Venus Williams to attend a tennis academy, they all relocated to Florida in 1991. Serena Williams began her professional career one year after her older sister, in 1995.

They quickly drew a lot of attention due to their powerful serves and ground strokes, as well as their outstanding athleticism. Many predicted that

Venus would be the first Williams sister to win a Grand Slam singles title, but Serena did so in 1999, when she won the U.S. Open. They both won the doubles event and also won 14 Grand Slam doubles titles all through their careers. Serena and Venus Williams won gold medals in the doubles event at the 2000 Olympic Games in Sydney, Australia.

Serena Williams asserted herself in 2002, winning the French Open, Wimbledon, and the US Open, defeating Venus Williams in the finals of all three tournaments. Serena Williams drew attention at the latter tournament by wearing a catsuit. Long interested in fashion, Williams became known for her daring ensembles that emphasized her strength while challenging traditional—and typically conservative—dress codes. With her trademark tenacity, Williams won the Australian Open in 2003, completing a career Grand Slam by winning all four component tournaments of the slam. She won Wimbledon later that year.

Williams won the Australian Open again in 2005. After suffering an injury, the following year, she won her third Australian Open in 2007. In 2008, the Williams won their second gold medal in doubles tennis at the Beijing Olympic Games. In

2009, She won her 10th Grand Slam singles title in the Australian Open. She also defeated her sister by winning her third Wimbledon singles title later that year. In 2010, Williams successfully defended her titles at the Australian Open and Wimbledon. She then battled a slew of health issues that kept her off the court for nearly a year.

Her fifth Wimbledon singles title was won in 2012. A month later, at the London Olympics, she won gold in the singles event, becoming only the second woman (after Steffi Graf) to complete a career Golden Slam. The sisters won the doubles event. Later that year, at the US Open, Williams won her 15th Grand Slam singles title. In 2013,

she won both her second and fifth French Open

singles and US Open singles titles respectively.

Williams then won the 2015 French Open, her

20th Grand Slam singles title. In 2016, She has

won 22 Grand Slam Singles in her career.

Williams announced in April 2017 that she was

pregnant (she had been engaged to Alexis

Ohanian, co-founder of the website Reddit, in

December 2016) and would miss the rest of the

2017 season. In September, Williams gave birth to

Olympia and then two months later, she married

Ohanian. In March, she resumed tennis but did

not win a tournament that year, despite reaching the finals of both Wimbledon and the US Open. Williams was penalized a game in the latter loss after arguing with the chair umpire about a code violation. In 2019, Williams Los in the finals of both Wimbledon and the US Open. Williams won her first singles event in three years at the 2020 ASB Classic in Auckland, New Zealand.

Williams reached the 2021 Australian Open semifinals before losing to Naomi Osaka. She was forced to withdraw from Wimbledon and the US Open later that year due to injuries. Williams competed at Wimbledon after missing the first half of the 2022 season but was defeated in the first round. She later revealed in an interview with Vogue magazine that she would be retiring after the upcoming US Open. Williams stated that she was transitioning away from tennis and toward other interests. Williams was also involved in activities off the court. She was particularly active in ventures involving fashion, beauty, and accessories.

CHAPTER TWO

<u>In Her Own Words, Serena Williams Says Goodbye to Tennis</u>

Williams stated in a first-person essay that she intends to retire from tennis after this year's U.S. Open. Williams insisted in her essay that she is not retiring. Instead, she claims to be evolving. Williams wrote, "I've never liked the word retirement." "It doesn't strike me as a modern word." I've been thinking of this as a transition, but I want to be careful how I use that word, which has a very specific and important meaning to a community of people. "Evolution may be the best word to describe what I'm up to."

As she approaches her 41st birthday in September, Williams appears to have concluded that the demands of tennis conflict with her other plans for her life. She wants to grow her family and expand her numerous business ventures, which include Serena Ventures, a venture capital firm that has raised $111 million and manages a portfolio of 60 start-ups.

It pains her to give up tennis. Williams wrote that she has been hesitant to admit to herself or anyone else that she must retire from tennis. She could not even discuss it with Alexis, her husband and her parents. Putting it all down to evolution, presumably, takes the sting out of her leaving a sport to which she has dedicated her life.

Who else could win a major championship while two months pregnant, as she did at the 2017 Australian Open? Who else could steal the show in a dynamic black catsuit at the French Open? (Williams' outfit at the 2018 tournament prompted the French Tennis Federation to outlaw catsuits.) Who else could study fashion design while at the pinnacle of her tennis career, then go on to launch successful clothing and jewelry lines? Who else could completely change people's perceptions of what older tennis players could achieve by winning 10 of her 23 Grand Slam titles after the age of 30? Who else could make strength appear so graceful? Williams' tennis resume alone ensures her GOAT status, but the impact she's made by using her voice so fearlessly propels her into icon territory.

Williams spoke out four years ago about the life-threatening complications she faced after doctors performed an emergency Cesarean section to give birth to her daughter. Williams was out of breath and told a nurse that she needed a CT scan based on her detailed knowledge of her medical history, but she was initially denied. She later informed her doctor, who thankfully listened to her. Doctors discovered she had several blood clots in her lungs at that time. Williams's public sharing of her ordeal became a powerful tool in the ongoing conversation about racial disparities in health care because black women are three times more likely than white women to die from pregnancy-related complications.

CHAPTER THREE

<u>Serena Williams as a Social Justice Advocate</u>

Williams fought for herself and dominated her sport without ever sacrificing her Blackness. When she was the world's sixth-ranked player in 2000, she backed out of a South Carolina event to support the NAACP's economic boycott of the state due to the Confederate flag flying at the statehouse. Williams wrote a heartfelt Facebook post in 2016 after two Black men, Alton Sterling and Philando Castile, were killed by police officers in separate incidents a day apart, about fearing for the life of her 18-year-old nephew.

Williams took on these fights for social justice

and equity voluntarily, despite being constantly

targeted by misogyny and racism. Some have

compared her to a monkey and a monster truck.

She's been referred to as a man, and she's been

subjected to racial slurs. Her defense against these

heinous assaults was to become the best player the

sport had ever seen. Her next challenge will be to

use her platform as effectively as she has

throughout her tennis career. Williams has been a

cultural icon for so long that it's difficult to

imagine her being anything less once she retires

from tennis. Watching her play has been inspiring

but seeing her grow will be even more so.

CHAPTER FOUR

Serena Williams postponed her retirement with a first-round victory at the US Open in 2022

It was Williams' third match since declaring her intention to "evolve away from tennis." Tickets for Monday's night session (August 29th, 2022) quickly became scarce after Williams announced her retirement. The cost of attending Monday's night session on a secondary ticket website was more than any previous US Open women's final.

Serena Williams opened singles play in the first round of the US Open at Arthur Ashe Stadium with a 6-3, 6-3 victory over Danka Kovini in what is likely her final tennis tournament. After struggling with her serve early on Monday, Williams won 10 of the final 13 games against Kovini, a 27-year-old Montenegrin ranked 80th in the world.

After the match, Williams said that the vocal crowd of nearly 24,000 people motivated her. Before improving her first serve percentage to 66%, she double-failed twice in the first game. Out of the 43 first serve points she faced, she won 33.

She was asked if this was her final tournament during her post-match press conference. "Yeah, I've been pretty vague about it, haven't I?" she asked, smiling. "I'll keep it vague because you never know." However, earlier on the court, Williams, 40, stated that moving on was a difficult decision. She said it's always difficult to walk away when one is passionate and love something so much. She also said it's sometimes more difficult to walk away than it is to stay.

Williams' singles victory was witnessed by her husband, Alexis Ohanian, and their daughter, Olympia, who wore white beads in her hair, similar to Williams' look like a teenager in 1999. She said she's looking forward to waking up and being able to choose what she has to do. She also can't wait to be a good mother to her daughter.

Williams will begin doubles play with her sister Venus on Wednesday, 31st of August. She will also play with Anett Kontaveit of Estonia, the second world best in the round 64 of singles. It will be their first professional meeting.